Mission Santa Inés

THE HIDDEN GEM

Text by Cresencia and Dale Olmstead
Photography by Jim Frank

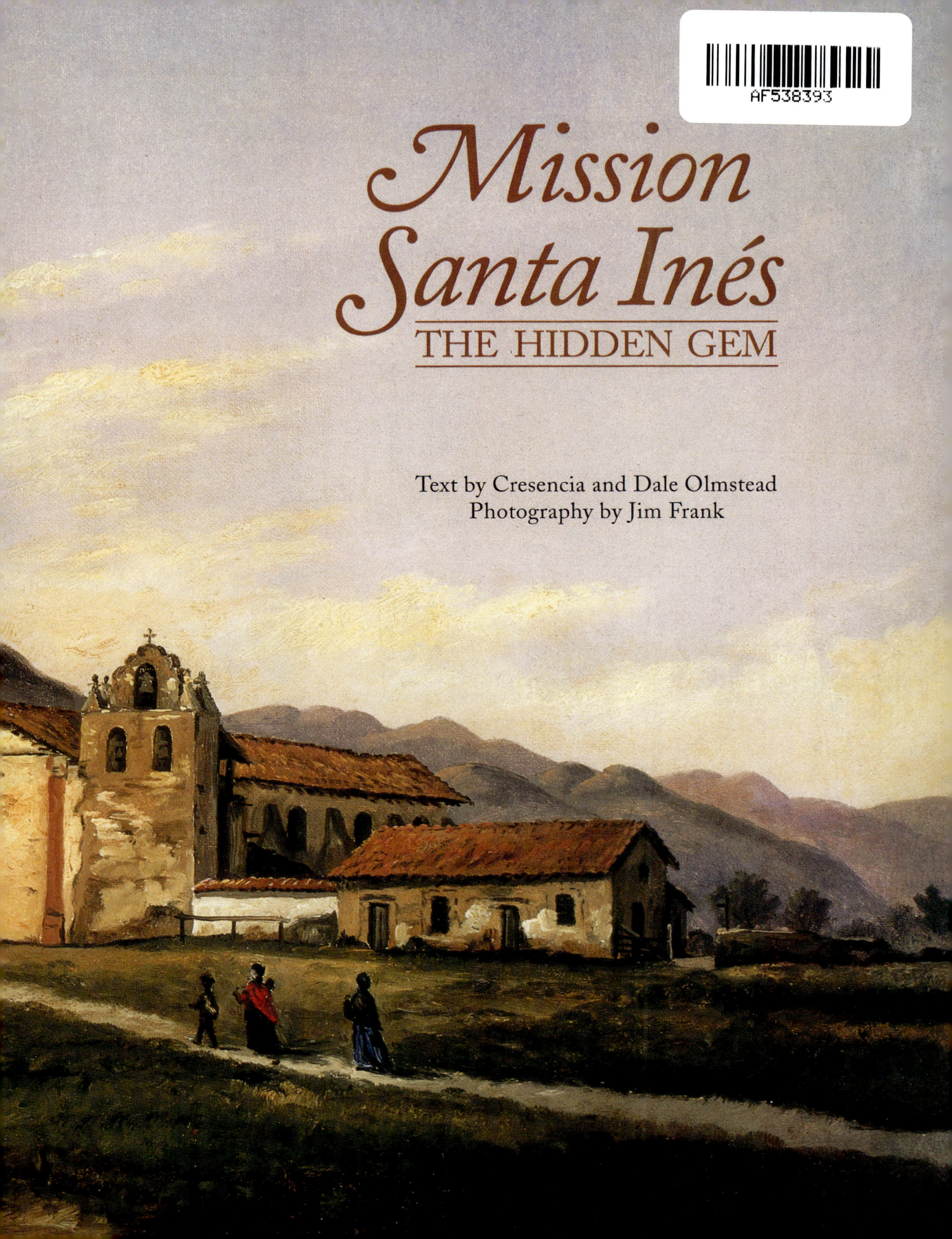

Welcome to Mission Santa Inés

Welcome to Mission Santa Inés, and allow me to introduce you to a true survivor. Mission Santa Inés overcame natural disasters, political turmoil, and financial hardships to emerge as one of the most successful of the southern California missions. Then the Mission endured rebellions, social upheaval, neglect, and decay only to rise again through restoration and repair as one of the hidden gems of the California mission chain.

The Mission was established in 1804 to serve the Chumash Indians in the Santa Ynez Valley area and to serve as a link between the missions in Santa Barbara and Lompoc. While still in its formative years, the Mission was devastated by the great earthquake of 1812. The Mission continued to rebuild and repair and actually became a very prosperous mission during the first part of the 19th century, when the Indian population was at its greatest. The Mission acreage produced plentiful harvests, and its livestock numbered in the thousands.

After Mexican independence from Spain, secularization caused the departure of the Spanish missionaries and the Indian neophytes, which nearly wiped out the Mission. It would have fallen into complete ruin were it not for the arrival of the Donahue family in 1882 and Father Alexander Buckler in 1904. Father Buckler began the repair of the Mission building and enlisted the talents of his niece to restore the art and artifacts. The Capuchin Franciscan Friars from Ireland, who followed them in 1924, continued their good works and efforts in this regard.

Today the process continues to restore, preserve, and return the "Mission of the Passes" to its former grandeur of the early mission era. Mission Santa Inés is the proud and fortunate possessor of a rich collection of paintings, statuary, vestments, manuscripts, and artifacts. The Mission, which commands a superb view of the Santa Ynez River Valley and the Santa Ynez and San Rafael mountain ranges, continues its central role in the spiritual and social life of the Santa Ynez Valley.

As you tour this picturesque Mission, may you be enriched spiritually by the drama, history, and tradition contained within the walls and grounds of Mission Santa Inés.

Fr. Richard J. Mahoney O.F.M. Cap.
Pastor, Mission Santa Inés

Regular religious services continue at the Mission and visitors are always welcome. A taped audio tour is available in our gift shop to guide visitors through the Museum rooms, church, and garden.

Contents

Library of Congress Number: 95-61321
ISBN: 0-9646858-0-9
Published by: Mission Santa Inés
P.O. Box 408
Solvang, California 93464
Produced by: Cachuma Press
P.O. Box 560
Los Olivos, California 93441
Text: Cresencia and Dale Olmstead
Photography (except where otherwise credited): Jim Frank
Reprints of historic photos: Bill Dewey
Graphic design: Katey O'Neill
Map: Sue Irwin
Printed in Singapore

Authors' Acknowledgments

We wish to express thanks and deep appreciation for articles contributed by Mike W. Loehr, Norman Neuerburg, and William Summers. Thank you to Teresa Brown, Erin Graffy de Garcia, and Catherine Piani for reading the manuscript, and to Father Virgilio Biasiol, O.F.M., for his moral support and for allowing use of resources at the Santa Barbara Mission Archive-Library. Finally, special thanks to Father Donal Burke, O.F.M. Cap., Mission Santa Inés, for his encouragement and support.

—Cresencia and Dale Olmstead, June 1995

***Cover:** Mission church and bell tower.* PHOTO BY JIM FRANK.
***Back cover:** Fountain in Mission garden.* PHOTO BY JIM FRANK.
***Title page:** Mission Santa Inés painted by Henry Chapman Ford, circa 1880.* COURTESY OF MISSION INN FOUNDATION AND MUSEUM, RIVERSIDE, CALIFORNIA.

Much of the beautiful Santa Ynez Valley looks as it did in pre-Mission times.

Chapter One

Pre-Mission History

Portuguese navigator Juan Rodriguez Cabrillo was credited with the discovery of the Santa Barbara Channel during an exploratory voyage in October 1542, in which he claimed the land in the name of the Spanish king. Sixty years later Sebastian Viscaíno named the channel in honor of Saint Barbara when he sailed in on the eve of the feast of St. Barbara, December 3, 1602.

In the following century, Franciscan missionaries joined the Spanish military in settling *alta* or upper California with the goal of a political and spiritual conquest of the new land. The Spanish missionary effort was to educate and convert the Indians to the Christian faith. As historian Maynard Geiger described it, "This was to be a cooperative effort, imperial in origin, protective in purpose, but primarily spiritual in execution."

The Chumash

The Spanish explorers and missionaries were quite taken with the Indians of the Santa Barbara Channel region—the Chumash. The peaceful natives impressed the explorers with their friendliness, hospitality, creative

Above: This mural in the Santa Barbara County Courthouse painted by Theodore Van Cina in 1929 depicts the landing of Juan Cabrillo on the Santa Barbara coast on October 13, 1542.
PHOTO BY BILL DEWEY.
Right: *Mural of Chumash daily life; one of four murals in the parish hall at Mission Santa Inés painted in 1994 by members of youth groups under the direction of Santa Ynez-area artists.*

abilities, and talents. The chaplain for the 1776 Anza Expedition, Father Pedro Font, described the Indians in his writings:

I surmise that these Indians who are so ingenious and so industrious, would become experts if they had teachers and suitable tools or implements, for they have nothing more than flints, and with them and their steady industry they make artifacts.

The Chumash populated a wide area—from Santa Paula to San Luis Obispo. They had a diversified and interdependent economy based on their many talents and craftsmanship. The Chumash even developed an excellent astronomical system, which was on a par with Europe in terms of accuracy. Their small, well-organized villages, called *rancherias* by the Spanish-speaking settlers, were made up of many large huts built from poles interwoven with reeds. The Indians gathered and leached acorns, and they also harvested nuts, seeds, and berries. They were skilled fishermen and enjoyed a variety of sea food, and they hunted animals as well. Although their only tool was flint, the resourceful Chumash created remarkably well-constructed sea-going plank canoes.

The New Mission: Site Selection

Previous to the founding of Mission Santa Inés, eighteen missions had been established, each one being approximately one day's journey from the next. The first, Mission San Diego, was founded in 1769 by Father Junípero Serra, followed by the establishment of other missions along the coast of California. After Father Serra's death, Father Fermín de Lasuén picked up the reins to continue the chain of missions.

The founding of a mission between La Purísima and Santa Barbara had been on the minds of the missionary fathers for several years. An inland mission north of Santa Barbara would solidify their work in the area; they would be able to take advantage of the Chumash Indians' already favorable disposition to being converted to Christianity. In addition, a very militant Indian tribe, the Tulares, lay to the northeast, just beyond the region controlled by the peaceful Chumash. A mission in the Santa Ynez Valley would secure the region as a buffer zone.

After completing the initial chain of missions to the north, Father Lasuén directed Father Estevan Tapis of Mission Santa Barbara to accompany Captain Felipe de Goycoechea to survey possible mission sites northeast of the coastal mountains. In the fall of 1798 the expedition surveyed the *Calahuasa* rancheria (presently the Santa Ynez Indian Reservation) and another Chumash site called *Alajulapu* (presently Solvang). Father Tapis reported that there were 325 dwellings at 14 sites at Calahuasa, so Lasuén requested Governor Diego Borica to recommend *Calahuasa* as a suitable site for a new mission.

It would be a number of years before the Franciscans were able to launch their new mission. The governor died, so approval was then needed from his successor, Jose de Arrillaga, in Baja California. Unfamiliar with the area, Governor Arrillaga wrote to Father Lasuén in April 1803 concerning the number of guards that would be needed for the new mission, but then Father Lasuén died.

In June of 1803 the new President of the Missions, Father Tapis, responded to Arrillaga's letter, detailing the number of Indians in the area and significant events such as the small group of Indian outlaws who had been committing murders throughout the region. In September the Father Guardian of the Franciscan order came from Mexico to survey the site and determined that a guard of six men would be sufficient to protect the mission.

Below: This painting by Russel Ruiz of a coastal Chumash village depicts reed dwellings as well as plank canoes used for fishing and travel between the Channel Islands and mainland. The Chumash also maintained inland village sites, including several in the Santa Ynez Valley. This painting is displayed at the Santa Barbara Mission Archive-Library. PHOTO BY BILL DEWEY.

Construction

In 1804 a row of buildings was constructed, measuring 232 feet in length and 19 feet in both height and width. This wing contained the temporary church (about 86 feet long), a sacristy (14 feet long) , the padres quarters (approximately 29 feet long), and the granary (103 feet long). With the aid of an initial group of Chumash converts from missions Santa Barbara and La Purísima Concepción, this portion was constructed six months prior to the formal founding of Mission Santa Inés. The 30-inch-thick walls were made of adobe (regional soil that contained much clay). The roof consisted of poles over which sticks were laid side by side, then covered with a layer of adobe soil that hardened, thus sealing out the elements.

On September 17, 1804 Father Tapis officially dedicated the mission to Saint Agnes. A temporary brushwood shelter was constructed at which 200 Indians attended solemn High Mass. Twenty-seven children were baptized and fifteen males enlisted for instruction. Fathers José Rumualdo Gutiérrez and José Antonio Calzada were selected as the first resident priests, and by the end of 1804 the Baptismal Register already contained the names of 112 Indian converts of all ages.

Below: "Old Mission Santa Inés," an oil painting made in 1882-1883 by Oriana Day. PHOTO COURTESY OF H. M. DE YOUNG MEMORIAL MUSEUM, GOLDEN GATE PARK, SAN FRANCISCO.

Treasures of Mission Santa Inés

The Vestments

Mission Santa Inés has the largest and most valuable collection of early California church vestments from the 15th century to 1718, having been the depository for vestments from the earlier successful missions in Baja California and Mexico. Many of the more than 500 silk vestments throughout the California missions are in fact older than the missions themselves. Father Junípero Serra noted this in 1769 when he collected them from missions in Baja California. Mission Santa Inés is also fortunate to have among its collection a vestment worn by Father Serra. That the vestments have been so well preserved is a tribute to the work of Mamie Goulet, the niece of Father Alexander Buckler (see page 20).

The vestments are made of materials such as beautiful oriental silks, with floral designs, satins, damasks, and brocades, which were transformed into Spanish- and Roman-style chasubles. Some have gold or silver flat threads woven into their designs.

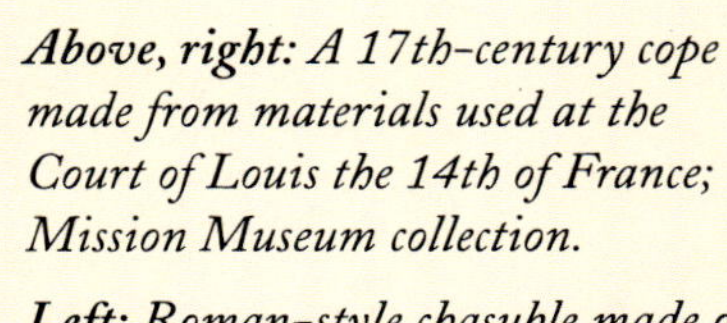

***Above, right:** A 17th-century cope made from materials used at the Court of Louis the 14th of France; Mission Museum collection.*

***Left:** Roman-style chasuble made of brocaded silk; Mission Museum collection.*

***Right:** A vestment worn by Father Junípero Serra; Mission Museum collection.*

Top, left: *Baptismal niche at the rear of the Mission Santa Inés church with statue of Saint John the Baptist and Indian-made (1812) hand-hammered zinc and copper baptismal font.*
Top, right: *Archangel Raphael, early 19th-century painting done by Indian neophyte; Mission Museum.*
Bottom: *Etching of Mission Santa Inés by Edward Borein done in the 1920s. The Mission Museum displays seven of his original works, including this one.* PHOTO BY BILL DEWEY.

Chapter Two

Early History
1804 to 1850

In the end-of-the-year report for 1805, Fathers Calzada and Gutiérrez stated that another row of buildings similar to the first one had been erected; it was 145 feet in length and 19 feet high and wide. In the report at the end of the following year in 1806, Fathers Caldaza and Taboada noted that another building had been added, 368 feet in length. To protect the walls from rain, a gallery or corridor covered with tiles was built measuring 75 feet long and 6 feet wide. By this time the quadrangle typical of the California missions had been completed at Mission Santa Inés—a square of about 350 feet on each side.

Although it was the last of the southern California missions, Mission Santa Inés was growing quickly because it could draw upon the support, tradition, and experience of the older, established missions. In 1807 new dwellings were constructed for the missionaries, and five double homes were built in 1810 for soldiers and their families, plus a storehouse and guardhouse.

Changes in the political air were soon to have their effect on mission life. After the beginning of the Mexican War of Independence against Spain in 1810,

support from Spain was no longer available to the missions, which meant their activities had to be self-supporting. Furthermore, soldiers were not receiving their wages and supplies regularly. This pushed the presidio commanders to become increasingly, if not unreasonably, dependent on the missions. The missions were to supply food and clothing to the soldiers, for which they were given IOU receipts.

The Earthquake of 1812

Eight years of accomplishment and growth were damaged or destroyed in just fifteen minutes at the end of 1812. The year-end report of Fathers Uria and Olbés included the following observation of the great earthquake of 1812:

December 21, 1812, at about 10 o'clock in the morning two earthquakes occurred at an interval of a quarter of an hour. The first made a considerable aperture in one corner of the church; the second shock threw down the said corner, and a quarter of the new houses contiguous to the church collapsed to the foundation. All the thin walls of the upper houses fell down, demolished all the tiles, and opened a main wall. All remain serviceable, however, if no greater tremors occur.

For safety, a temporary church was erected outside the quadrangle area. Reconstruction of the damaged buildings continued over the next four years, and a new and larger church facing east was built of adobe and brick. It measured 140 feet long, 25 feet wide, and 30 feet high, with heavily buttressed walls 5 feet thick. Heavy pine timbers brought from the San Rafael Mountains supported its ceiling and retiled roof. The ceiling height was lowered on the residence of the friars, and the flat roof replaced with a gabled roof covered with tiles. These buildings, which were dedicated on July 4, 1817, are all that remain of the Mission from that era.

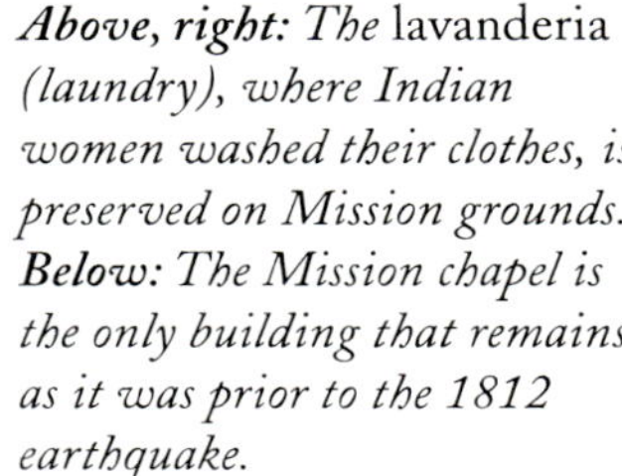

Above, right: *The* lavanderia *(laundry), where Indian women washed their clothes, is preserved on Mission grounds.* ***Below:*** *The Mission chapel is the only building that remains as it was prior to the 1812 earthquake.*

Rebuilding: Progress and Productivity

Despite these early struggles, the California mission effort was developing and succeeding. The large communities of Indian converts allowed for the development of vast herds of cattle, and some missions successfully raised ample acreage of grains, fruits, and other produce. The missions were virtually at the peak of their productivity in the early 19th century. An 1817 inventory of Mission Santa Inés listed possessions of 6,000 head of cattle, 5,000 sheep, 120 goats, 150 pigs, 120 pack mules, and 770 horses. In that year, Mission Santa Inés lands produced 4,160 bushels of wheat, 4,330 bushels of corn, and 300 bushels of beans. The Mission baptismal book in 1817 recorded 1,030 names, most of which were Indian. Also recorded were 287 marriages and 611 deaths. The Mission registered its greatest Indian population that same year, with a total of 920 Native Americans.

From 1808 until 1824, Father Uria continually pushed an ambitious building program. In the initial years of the Mission, he oversaw the development of housing for the missionaries and soldiers, as well as the construction of the storehouse. After the earthquake of 1812, he supervised the reconstruction of the church. It was Uria who saw to it that the church interior was decorated with murals between 1818 and 1820. He also directed the construction of the new grist mill and reservoirs in 1820; they were built with massive walls to avoid damage from future earthquakes. In 1824, the church interior was freshly painted and redecorated. During this year, numerous paintings and other church artifacts were acquired that can be seen in the Mission today.

Above, left: *Many of the Mission quadrangle structures collapsed in 1884, and the buttressed arch in the parking area (known as the 19th arch) is all that remains of the southern end of the Mission.* ***Above:*** *One of the early-era Mission reservoirs is situated in front of the Mission church and bell tower.*

Joseph Chapman and the Pirates

Mission Santa Inés is closely linked to the adventurous life of Joseph Chapman, one of the earliest Anglo settlers in California.

Originally from Maine, Joseph Chapman eventually came to Hawaii in 1818. During this time, the French pirate Hippolyte de Bouchard was sailing against Spain. After raiding the Philippines, he too arrived in Hawaii. Bouchard acquired an additional ship and an unwilling crew, including Joseph Chapman, and sailed for Spanish settlements in California in October 1818. Military and civilians were alerted up and down the coast to watch for the pirates. After a stop in Monterey, Bouchard's group sailed

Treasures of Mission Santa Inés

Music Manuscripts

The six music manuscripts that survive from the mission period in the Mission Santa Inés Archive are important testaments to the musical activity of the Franciscan friars and the Native Americans who used these manuscripts for the Mission choir and orchestra. The surviving music manuscripts give us a glimpse of the importance of singing at all of the missions.

The six manuscripts and fragments of the originals are but a part of the choral library of the Mission. The musical content is primarily "plainsong," also called Gregorian chant, which is one-line, homophonic music sung to Latin texts. The beautifully produced manuscripts exemplify the book production practices used by the Roman Catholic Church since the Middle Ages.

Left: Mission music manuscript of a Gregorian chant, 1841.

Above: Remains of the milling complex built in the 1820s, about a half mile east of the Mission.

south to Santa Barbara. The pirates found the Ortega Ranch in Refugio Canyon conveniently deserted when they arrived, so they plundered the ranch and set it on fire. Sergeant Carlos Antonio Carrillo and his men lay in wait to ambush Bouchard outside Refugio. Chapman and several others were captured by the squad of soldiers.

Bouchard sailed to Santa Barbara under a flag of truce and asked the Presidio for an exchange of prisoners. In the process, Chapman somehow ended up freed from Bouchard, but was held as a temporary prisoner in the Presidio. Upon his release, he became a model citizen. He was baptized as a Catholic at Mission San Buenaventura and later married Guadalupe Ortega (of the Ortega Ranch) at Mission Santa Inés. Chapman and his wife moved to Santa Ynez, where he was employed at the Mission. In 1821 Chapman constructed the Mission's fulling mill (for treating woolen garments), which was built near the grist mill.

Chumash Revolt

In 1821 Mexico won its independence from Spain and two years later became its own republic. Although good news for Mexico, this initiated a difficult period for the missions. Since the Mexicans identified the missions with the imperialism of Spain, the missions were ignored and allowed to deteriorate.

The missions already were owed thousands of pesos of IOUs from the presidios. Antagonism grew as the soldiers compelled the mission Indians to work overtime without pay over the objections of the mission fathers. Ill-tempered and discontented because they themselves were without pay and supplies, many soldiers allowed their frustrations to affect the way they treated the Indians. In 1824 events and emotions were pushed to the boiling point.

A Spanish guard at Santa Inés flogged a Purísima Indian, setting off a revolt that touched all the Santa Barbara area missions. In the revolt against the Santa Inés soldier guards, two Indians were killed, several buildings were set on fire, and the priests became unwitting hostages with the soldiers' families with whom they took initial refuge. The revolt lasted several months, and before it was over fourteen Chumash lives were lost, including the two at Santa Inés. The Indians rightly feared reprisal from the soldiers and fled from the missions to hide.

Ultimately, the Indians had no quarrel with the padres, whom they treated with deference and respect. However, the natives made it clear to the padres that the soldiers' attitudes and behavior were the reasons for the uprising. The Chumash felt that since they had worked on behalf of the soldiers without any pay and for an inordinate amount of time, they should have been treated with the utmost kindness, gratitude, and dignity. Instead they received arrogant disrespect and derision. During the revolt, the soldiers had unnecessarily destroyed some of the Indians' homes and possessions. The padres did not condone the actions of the Indians, but were quick to call the behavior of the Presidio personnel unreasonable, and in some cases inexcusable, especially the unjustifiable killings of the Indians.

Secularization

The ratification of Mexico's Secularization Laws in 1834 caused the mission system to rapidly draw to a close. The Mexican legislative assembly had passed a decree allowing the mission properties to become "secularized" over the following ten years. This meant the missions were to be transferred from the jurisdiction of the missionaries of religious orders (which were mostly Spanish in California) to a bishop who would administer them through diocesan or "secular" priests (not part of a religious order). In effect, the Mexicans were trying to eliminate the Spanish

Top: Many early-era architectural details, such as this beautiful door handle, can be appreciated at today's Mission.
Bottom: *The cemetery is located behind the Mission bell tower. The first entry in the burial register is dated January 23, 1805.*

influence; the missions were then reduced to parish churches.

The problem with this was that in many cases there were no secular personnel or diocesan personnel available to run the missions. As a "parish church" Mission Santa Inés had no governmental support. The Mission fathers initially maintained themselves from the income gained from the sale of cattle, tallow, hides, and from what grain could be harvested.

The resulting conditions were disheartening for the Indians, who received little or no recompense for their labors and were required to pay the salary of the secular "administrators." The result was that many Chumash simply fled. This aggravated the decline of the mission system, since there were no longer enough Indians to attend to the crops and cattle and maintain the buildings.

California's First College Seminary

In 1843 Governor Manuel Micheltorena tried to halt the secularization. He had about 35,500 acres of land transferred from Mission Santa Inés to Francisco Garcia Diego y Moreno, the first Bishop of Alta California. This land grant was used to establish the first college seminary in California. Originally situated in the Mission Santa Inés compound in 1844, the college seminary later moved to the College Ranch near Santa Ynez where it continued to educate priests and the general public until it closed in 1881.

The sympathetic Micheltorena was replaced in 1846 by Governor Pio Pico, whose policies accelerated the despoiling of the missions. In June of 1846 he illegally sold Mission Santa Inés to José M. Covarrubias and José Joaquin Carrillo for $7,000, just three weeks before the United States took control of California.

Fathers J. J. Jimeno and Francisco Sánchez continued in charge of the college seminary until May 7, 1850 when they surrendered the management of Mission Santa Inés to priests of the Congregation of the Sacred Hearts of Jesus and Mary (Picpus Fathers of South America). The arrival and brief stay of the Picpus Fathers at Mission Santa Inés marked the end of Franciscan management and the mission period.

Below and right: *These murals depicting early Mission life were painted by members of various youth groups under the direction of Santa Ynez-area artists in 1994. They are displayed in the parish hall of Mission Santa Inés.*

Treasures of Mission Santa Inés

Paintings and Statues

Mission Santa Inés, in spite of being one of the last missions to be founded, today possesses a remarkably large collection of paintings from the mission period, as well as a number of statues.

The painting of *Saint Agnes* in the Mission Museum was done by Andres Lopez in Mexico City in 1803 and was sent soon after to the Mission.

One of the most important paintings is *The Archangel Raphael* (see page 10), currently on display in the Mission Museum. It is the only mission-period painting on canvas by a native convert, other than a set of *Stations of the Cross* housed at another mission.

The fourteen *Stations of the Cross* in the church are based on an engraved series copied from the church of Santa Maria del Giglio in Venice.

Significant statues at Mission Santa Inés include *Saint Agnes* in the niche above the main altar, and the *Virgin of the Rosary* in the area that had previously been a doorway to the cemetery.

The decorations in the church were done under the direction of skilled artisans who had access to old pattern books of neoclassical design. The skillfully executed architectural and floral decorations include the particularly fine floral and Greek key pattern in the sacristy. Designs outside the altar rail appear to have been done by neophyte artists. All the original designs (1818-1820) had survived untouched until they were restored and repainted in the 1970s.

Above, left: Saint Vibiana, *patron saint of the Archdiocese of Los Angeles, oil on canvas, 19th-century Mexican painting.*
Above, right: Our Lady of the Rosary, *an excellent Mexican Baroque-period sculpture from the mid-18th century.*
Below: *One of fourteen* Stations of the Cross *paintings in the chapel; late 18th century, oil on canvas, from the College of Guadalupe at Zacatecas, Mexico.*

Chapter Three

A New Era
1851 to the Present

Father Eugene O'Connell succeeded the Picpus Fathers in the summer of 1851. He made various improvements that included laying the first asphalt floors, some of which can still be seen in the garden area.

In 1851 the United States government rescinded the illegal sale of the Mission lands by Pio Pico. A decree signed by President Lincoln on May 23, 1862 formally returned the missions to the Catholic Church, with possession given to the Bishop of Monterey, since the Franciscans were no longer at the Mission.

In 1877 supervision of the college seminary was transferred to the Christian Brothers, who remained until 1881 when financial problems led to their departure. The Bishop sold off 20,000 acres, reducing Mission Santa Inés to less than half of its size, with 16,000 acres remaining.

In 1882 the Donahue family came from Ireland to live at the Mission. For 16 years they resided in the southern half of the rectory and, despite a lack of funds, set themselves to the task of making repairs and reroofing. However, the scope of repairing the quickly deteriorating structures was beyond any one family. The southern

Above, left: Mamie Goulet and unknown soldier displaying one of the many vestments she restored. SANTA BARBARA MISSION ARCHIVE-LIBRARY.
Above, right: Father Alexander Buckler. SANTA INÉS MISSION ARCHIVE.
Below: This photo of ruins at Mission Santa Inés may date from as early as 1865. SANTA BARBARA MISSION ARCHIVE-LIBRARY.

section of the front corridor collapsed in 1884, and soon the adjacent building fell into ruin, leaving only the buttressed arch, currently preserved within the parking area.

Father Alexander Buckler

A new period began for Mission Santa Inés in July of 1904, when diocesan priest Father Alexander Buckler became pastor with jurisdiction over the outlying stations of Lompoc, Sisquoc, and Las Cruces.

He began a concerted effort to maintain and restore the Mission buildings and their contents. Besides addressing the basic needs of better shelter, he constructed a water and drainage system and reinforced much of the padres' crumbling quarters. Father Buckler had the church and parts of the rectory reroofed and removed the crumbling adobes at the rear. During an exceptionally heavy rainstorm in 1911, the bell tower, already weakened from age, collapsed. The following year Father Buckler rebuilt it and added a third arch.

Among the most cherished possessions of the Mission are the vestments. Father Buckler sought the assistance of his niece, Miss Mamie Goulet, to repair the vestments, as well as some of the paintings and statuary.

When Father Buckler retired in November 1924, an offer was made to return Mission Santa Inés to the Franciscans. The Franciscan superior declined to accept, so the offer was extended to the Capuchin Franciscan Order of the Irish Province.

The Capuchin Franciscans

A first concern of the Capuchin Franciscans was the installation of electric lighting and modern plumbing to improve living conditions at the Mission. The inner garden of the Mission was given a more formal appearance in 1926, with the planting of a hedge in the shape of a Celtic cross.

The Capuchins began full restoration of the Mission in 1947. When workmen removed the roof from part of the building, they discovered several rooms that had been used as living quarters in the previous century by the Mission fathers. This revealed an open balcony with rooms behind it above the arches. Extensive repairs were made to the roof of the church and the rectory, and sections of the south end of the building were thoroughly remodeled.

This project restored the building to its two-story condition as it might have appeared prior to the earthquake of 1812. The bell tower was remodeled to conform to its original design, as confirmed by artwork and photographs, prior to its collapse in 1911. Red tile flooring unearthed during the project affirmed that the Mission edifice originally had 22 arches, and not 21 as previously believed. A Mission bell was shipped to Rotterdam for recasting, returning in time to ring out in celebration of the 150th anniversary of Mission Santa Inés in 1954.

Above, left and right: *Wall details, showing results of restoration painting that took place in the 1970s. Left image includes 18th-century colonial silver monstrance from Mexico.* SANTA BARBARA MISSION ARCHIVE-LIBRARY.

Left: *The expansive garden behind the Mission is a lovely surprise for many visitors. Dating to the Mission's earliest days, the garden has undergone many changes; it currently retains the formal design of a hedge in the shape of a Celtic cross implemented by the Capuchin Franciscans in 1926.*

The Chapel of the Madonnas was created during this period and numerous restoration projects were initiated. A radiation heating system was installed in the church under the original restored tile floor to preserve the Mission's priceless paintings and other artwork by moderating the damp conditions. The entire Mission was painted and weatherproofed. Improved irrigation and drainage systems were installed for the various refurbished and relandscaped gardens. In 1954 a statue of Our Lady of Lourdes made in Obergammergau was installed in the shrine next to the cemetery.

Foundation stones of the original Mission quadrangle may still be found at the northwest corner of the Mission grounds. The original quadrangle, which measured 350 feet square with walls 20 feet high, contained all that was necessary for the Mission at that time: a tannery, blacksmith and potter's shops, facilities for weaving and basketmaking, a soap factory, and other work areas. Two new bronze bells named "Santa Inés" and "Saint Francis" were cast and installed in the bell tower in 1984.

In August of 1989 the 18th annual Fiesta celebrated many years of hard work—in particular the culmination of a million-dollar renovation and restoration project for the east wing. Key to this project was the reconstruction of eight of the nineteen arches that form the eastern facade of the building. This recreated the Mission's facade as it would have appeared prior to its secularization by the Mexican government in 1834. Restoration efforts of the Mission paintings became a focus in 1992 and are ongoing.

***Top:** Fathers Kelleher and O'Leary examine adobe walls during renovation work in 1949.* SANTA INÉS MISSION ARCHIVE.
***Above, right:** The Thomas J. Donahue family lived at the Mission from 1882 to 1902 and were responsible for much restoration work on the Mission buildings.* VIRGINIA R. DAYS' COLLECTION.
***Right:** This is the restored arched colonade in front of the Mission.*

Treasures of Mission Santa Inés

The Bells

Bells have always played an important role in the life of the Mission, calling early members to prayer or work, marking the time of day, tolling for the deceased, joyfully celebrating the union of marriages, ringing out the traditional "Angelus," and noting the end of day. The bells of Santa Inés have rung out across the valley since September 17, 1804. On that day a cross was planted and the bell was suspended from a neighboring oak tree. The Mission's first bell site was destroyed by the earthquake of 1812.

During 1814 to 1816, a large adobe wall was constructed to hold three bells. New bells were cast in Lima, Peru, and the formal dedication took place on July 4, 1817. The bell wall lasted until 1911 when a huge rainstorm literally melted it. When Father Buckler had it rebuilt the following year, a third bell arch was added.

The Mission museum displays four bells. The 1804 Juan Baptisia bell is the oldest. The Ave Maria Purísima bell was cast in 1807, and the bell from Lima was cast in 1817. Still hanging in the top arch of the bell wall is the 1818 Lima bell, which was recast in 1953. The 1912 St. Agnes bell was used for the dedication of the new tower that same year. Two new bells were dedicated in 1984.

Top: *1818 Lima bell in top arch of tower.*
Above, left: *Mission Santa Inés bell tower.*
Right: *The Ave Maria Purísima bell, cast in 1807, is displayed in the Mission Museum.*

A Living Tradition

Mission Santa Inés continues as an active parish church of approximately 1,000 families. It holds regular religious services as well as special services for baptisms, confirmations, weddings, and funerals. The Mission staff conducts religious education classes, youth groups, and various programs for adults.

Community groups are allowed to use Mission facilities for public functions such as the annual Story Telling Festival and the yearly *Rancheros Vistadores* horse-riding event, and the Mission grounds are used as the staging area for parades and cycling events. The popular annual Fiesta benefits restoration work at the historic Mission.

Top: *Wedding in the Mission chapel.*
Above, left: *Fiesta dancers pose in the Mission gardens.*
Above, right: Los Rancheros Vistadores *start their annual ride at the Mission grounds.*
Left: *Virgin of Guadalupe illuminated for Holy Day.*